T0105848

LOOKING FOR BIGFOOT,

FINDING ONLY MYSELF

AN INTROSPECTIVE LENS ON THE SOUL

A LIGHTENED SELF-STUDY

BY **H. R. DAVIS**

EDITED BY JOSEPH S. BENSON PHD

BALBOA.PRESS

A DIVISION OF HAY HOUSE

Balboa Press books may be ordered through booksellers or by contacting:

Balboa Press
A Division of Hay House
1663 Liberty Drive
Bloomington, IN 47403
www.balboapress.com
844-682-1282

Print information available on the last page.

ISBN: 979-8-7652-4270-4 (sc)
ISBN: 979-8-7652-4271-1 (e)

Library of Congress Control Number: 2023909908

Balboa Press rev. date: 05/25/2023

FROM THE AUTHOR

From my experience, writing a book doesn't mean just sitting down and typing. There's a whole process and it isn't always easy. For this book especially, there was almost a year of planning for the journey that took place. There were books and research articles to read, sightings to find and map out and countless conversations with friends, family and acquaintances along the way. There was a move involve, so there was a moving company, a couple realtors and finance companies. This isn't just a book about a story, this is a chapter of my life and nothing is as simple as just getting into the car. There are a few important people that need to be acknowledged for their help along the way.

For my Editor who is also a very close friend, thank you for immediately jumping on board with the idea of this endeavor. Your collaboration, anecdotes, suggestions and your keen eye are much appreciated. Your unwavering dedication to my craft is like gasoline on a fire. A fire that is continually burning all of my free time and energy.

I have to recognize my former supervisor and friend, Mr. Eric. You probably don't realize how much you inspire me to look for bigfoot. Your constant banter and support make you a fine leader and a mentor for me. I would like to note that even though you were furious about this move, you still supported my adventure. For that I appreciate you.

For my mother, who passed during the very beginnings of the planning of this book, thank you always for your continued belief that I can do anything. You always believed in me, even when I didn't believe in myself.

For all my friends and family, your encouragement and support throughout this journey and every other journey in my life is inspiring. I know many of you are living vicariously through my life sometimes, but your continued love helps me keep it all real.

For my readers (I don't believe I have a fan-following yet) I appreciate your support. Please continue to buy my books so I can buy new shoes.

INTRODUCTION

The older I get, the more I realize that I need less and less to make me happy and content. Give me good food, good company and a good story and I'm set. I started planning for this book long before I started writing it. As soon as I decided that I was going to move from Virginia to Louisiana, I started planning for the trip. Once I started planning for the trip, I started planning this book. What started as a farce – a cryptid hunt across half the country – became a work in self-study. I didn't want to write a critical self-analysis study. I had my chance at doing a dissertation and passed it up. So I decided to do a comparative project, looking at myself through the lens of cryptozoology. It's less academic, more charming and a ton more fun. I had hoped to gain insight into my love for travel, mythology and all things out of the ordinary. What I learned was that 90 percent of the time, I care more about my next meal than where I'm laying my head at night.

By creating a pseudo-study with myself as the only subject, I was able to keep this content light enough for the average reader, but also spark some intrigue for those who might want to read further. Unlike my other books, which are purely fiction, this book is non-fiction. The places and feelings and ponderings are real, true and my own. The journey is not fictional, the food was very real, nothing was created or elaborated. I kept a journal for over a year. I recorded findings, experiences, thoughts, events, and interpretations. I applied a critical lens of any good researcher. I grounded myself in the research that already exists, but since this is not a dissertation, but rather an entertaining retelling, I didn't bother to do a literature review of the existing publications on self-study.

I analyzed my travel journal through two lenses: introspection and cryptozoology. By turning the lens on myself, I was able to become more self-aware and even look at my journal and my findings objectively. By focusing on a cryptid overlay of the data, I was able to compare myself, not with those who have researched cryptids before, but rather I was able to compare myself with a cryptid directly.

In doing all this, I have created something that isn't research, but also isn't fiction. It isn't just a story, though. This is more of a journey providing context into my life, my thoughts, my feelings, my hungers and my perspectives on the world around me.

This book in no way represents a claim that any cryptid exists. It may provide insight for me and possibly for some readers into why we feel the need to believe in things like bigfoot or God, or BBQ that is existential.

Buckle into the passenger seat, come along for the journey and the hunt. Maybe you'll learn to use an introspective lens on your own journey. Maybe you'll begin to see yourself in the position of your favorite cryptid. Maybe you'll just share some laughs along the way, or maybe you'll be completely offended, and that's ok too. If you had to think about anything that follows, I've succeeded in my purpose.

PART ONE

A QUANDARY AND AN ADVENTURE

CHAPTER ONE

THE BEGINNING AND PREPARING FOR THE BEGINNING IN THAT ORDER

B EFORE ONE BEGINS A SEARCH, I should think it might be important to know what he or she is searching for. I've searched for trivial things like shoes, my keys, the TV remote and a missing sock. Finding your keys on the hook by the door, exactly where they should be, after an hour of looking all over the house could hardly be considered a search, though. Or, if that is a search, then what I've done is much, much more. I went searching for Bigfoot. Perhaps that statement is too strong. Let me rephrase… I went on a journey and searched for Bigfoot along the way. Maybe that isn't exactly accurate either. I went on an adventure, a partly necessary journey; on the way, I didn't search for bigfoot, I searched for habitats, food and shelter, that could potentially, in my mind's eye, support a creature such as bigfoot. Though having no real idea what bigfoot might require, I thought about whether or not I, a full size (if not slightly plus size) man could find shelter and food in the habitats I explored. The idea being that if I could potentially survive in said habitats, a larger, hairier version of myself might also survive there.

In 1930, my grandpa, my dad's dad, fresh out of high school in the midst of the Great Depression, set out on a journey from Kansas to the West Coast searching for work. He went north, then west, sending letters home all along the way. I have those letters and I've traced his steps, I've journeyed his path. That's a book I haven't written yet. However, his story, his journey, his search has always inspired me, made me restless, made me curious. His journey may have brought him nearer to Bigfoot than I'll ever be. He spent months in the Pacific Northwest where Bigfoot sightings abound. I've always dreamed of just taking off one summer and renting an RV, driving up and down mountains, through redwood groves and through all sorts of back country searching for Bigfoot in the Pacific Northwest.

That's another trip, yet another book, another wandering, another set of questions, another adventure, another discovery, another journey. This journey, this adventure, this search begins on the East Coast in the city of Norfolk, Virginia. This journey goes through the back country of North Carolina, back to Virginia, through Tennessee, Kentucky, Alabama, Mississippi, and Louisiana following recent sightings, hiking back country trails, exploring mountains, hills, caves and swamps. The journey continued north through Arkansas, Oklahoma, and Eastern Kansas and back to Louisiana. I even took a detour to Greece, a country rich with mythology full of monsters, half monsters and adventures. I looked at terrain and analyzed whether I thought a large mammal could survive in the wild everywhere I went. I observed food and water sources, hiding places, and interactions a creature that size might have with humans and other life forms.

RESEARCHER POSITIONING – MY PLACE
IN A BLACK HOLE OF LITERATURE

As a trained researcher, I know how to look at data. I specialized in qualitative, narrative and historical research. I've taken and passed my quantitative research classes as well. I can run the numbers when needed, but mostly, when I'm looking at the data, I'm looking at the narrative, the historical record of similar narratives and how those narratives and histories add to the human experience. Question my credentials if you want, I would, but it matters little. I'm not adding to any volume of research, I'm simply reporting what I saw and experienced on my journeys.

What I didn't expect this journey to be was a reflective self-study. In fact, though I've read some on self-study, I had never given it much merit as a methodology. I suppose that's how it always goes. You search for your missing sock and find the missing Tupperware lid instead. You look for your birth certificate and find your first grade report cards. (It appears I may have been smarter back then).

I don't claim to be a smart man. I can write, I can read and I can use a calculator. I've spent the majority of my life in school. I have an Associate's Degree, two Bachelor's Degrees, a Master's Degree and I nearly finished my Doctorate Degree. My written and oral comprehensive exams focused on Identity Theory and Social Identity Theory. I'm well educated which is not the same as being smart. A smart man would figure out how to amass vast amounts of money and live comfortably without paying an exorbitant amount of money for an education that continuously fails to bring me, I mean them, said amounts of money.

ON THE QUANDRY OF WANDERINGS —
A BASIS FOR WANDERLUST

If I'm being honest, since leaving home to go to college, I've never really felt like anywhere was home again. After my parents moved from my childhood home and it was dozed down, I've never felt like there was ever a home to go back to. I mean, yes, my parents moved to another house and it became their home, but I don't guess it was ever my home, even though I lived there for a year as an adult. It occurs to me that there are very few houses or even places where I've lived for more than a couple years since moving out of my parent's. I've never felt settled. Even when I moved further away, I never found a house that I could call home. In five years living several hours away, I lived in seven houses. When I returned to my "home" corner of Kansas, I still lived in several places while working on my doctorate degree. When I got the opportunity to move to California, I jumped on it, and then I picked up and moved 18 months later all the way across the country to Virginia. Three years in Virginia equated to 3 different houses. I've been to 34 states in the US. I'm only missing the New England states, Alaska and Hawaii. I've been to 20 foreign countries. I've never been "settled."

A REASON FOR JOURNEY —
AN EXCUSE TO WRITE

I never saw this wandering as important until I started on this book, this adventure, this journey of discovery. It should be a surprise to no one that knows me that this book starts as I prepared to make yet another life move. Though I loved my life in Virginia, I had the opportunity to move to New Orleans, Louisiana. Opportunity to see and live and experience a new place always wins out over stability and the same old commute to work. If there's anything we learned from COVID, it's that commutes are overrated.

Anytime I travel, I like to add another dimension to the trip by making it a themed trip. Once I drove across the American Southwest and ONLY stayed at old vintage motels with neon lights where I picked up a serious case of crabs and played connect the dots with the bullet holes in the wall. I never said I was a smart man. I am fairly adventurous though. Another time I planned a beer trip. I planned my destinations around local breweries and I'm not sure how I made it home without a DUI. While it sounded fun, I didn't bring a designated driver. That was poor planning on my part, again, I'm educated, that doesn't mean I'm smart. Other trips have included Safari trips where I stopped at drive-thru safaris and wildlife preserves and local diner trips where I only ate at small town locally run diners.

For this move from Norfolk, Virginia to New Orleans, Louisiana, I decided I was going to do a cryptid themed trip. I would head west and then south, hitting West Virginia, Ohio, Tennessee, Kentucky, Alabama, Mississippi and Louisiana. There were so many things to see along this route; Mothman, Lizardman, Bigfoot, the Wampus Cat, the Ozark Howler, Hogzilla, and more. I spent two months planning a route that went through small towns where recent sightings had been reported. There were caves to explore, mountains to cross, woods to hike through, parks to visit, small towns to see and I had plenty of time to make the trip happen.

Just as I started coordinating everything with cross country movers, and getting things packed and ready for the trip, circumstances changed which delayed my trip by over 2 months. I would now be leaving in early December, instead of mid-September. Normally, that wouldn't be much of an issue, except that crossing the Blue Ridge and Appellation Mountains in December can be a bit tricky. Every great traveler plans for changes in the plans. Every smart man knows that sometimes your plans get turned upside down. I am an educated man and an experienced traveler – I'm not a great traveler nor a smart man.

As a trial run for my research for this trip, I took a short trip just south of Virginia into North Carolina. I would do a bit of research on large mammals in the Outer Banks. The wild Corolla horses are large mammals living in sandy scrub brush on an island off the coast of North Carolina. Looking at how large land mammals like horses survive with extremely limited fresh water and only woody scrub brush and sand grass to eat might shed some light on how a large creature like bigfoot could survive in the wild remote wilderness of North America.

Knowing I wanted to write a book out of this adventure, I purchased a journal and a very nice set of pens. I would keep a journal all along the way, writing my thoughts, sharing my experiences and analyzing everything about the places I would visit, searching for habitat I deemed able to support a creature such as bigfoot.

Having only overly dramatized information about bigfoot gathered from conspiracy theory type documentaries, I purchased several seemingly credible books about bigfoot and other cryptids. I could at the very least educate myself on what I hoped to see along the way. I searched the internet for sightings, plotted my route and mapped out state and national parks, nature preserves and protected lands where humans would be scarcer and wildlife would be more abundant. In my mind, that allowed a greater chance for an encounter.

I identified several potential weakness in my research. I was travelling in December. While large mammals further south may not hibernate for the winter months, many certainly do in the mountains. I realized that I may not encounter any wildlife in the wintery mountains. I was also going to be relatively limited on time. I was, after all, coordinating with interstate movers to get my household goods moved as well. I didn't have a place to stay in Louisiana upon my arrival yet either. I needed to put some miles on the car, get down south and find lodging so my household goods could be delivered. I figured I had about 14 days I could spend on the road. That would limit the amount of time I could spend hiking in the woods, talking to locals and driving backroads.

Nevertheless, an adventure was coming and no matter what, I was going to go and I was going to document the trip and when I found bigfoot, I was going to be ready with camera in hand. Bigfoot and I would be insta-famous, or something.

CHAPTER TWO

NORTH CAROLINA

THE TRIAL RUN — CONTROL EXPERIMENT

AS A CONTROL EXPERIMENT, I went somewhere close to home and somewhere well documented for having large land animals surviving in unlikely habitat. If I could look at the wild horses of the Outer Banks and collect narrative data from locals, tour guides and my personal observation, I might be able to make some educated assumptions about whether or not a large animal like bigfoot might also be able to exist with limited resources. My research wanderings were as follows: By comparison, can large mammals of unknown species but perhaps of similar size theoretically survive in similar conditions as the wild horses of Corolla, North Carolina? Is it possible that said large unknown species might go largely undetected in similar conditions as the wild horses of Corolla, North Carolina?

DECEMBER 1, 2021

The search begins. I barely left home, started the search for bigfoot today. I didn't see anything out of the ordinary, but I did find a super awesome BBQ place on the side of the road on the Virginia and North Carolina border, just outside the Dismal Swamp.

I posted a picture of cardboard food dish with red and white gingham paper, piled high with slow smoked brisket smothered – no, drowned – in smoky sweet homemade barbecue sauce. I had not anticipated such finger licking goodness to come from a small rickety shack on the side of the road. One stood on old pallets to keep out of the mud while ordering from a menu hand-scrawled on a blackboard, barely legible. The woods just behind the shack were filled with the smoke of what I can only guess was a huge homemade pit, dripping with pig juice and bovine trimmings, all prepared for me by what I imagined to be a half blind ancient pit master who cannot see the meat, but rather smells it and has an extra sensory knowledge of cooked carcasses, letting him (or her) know exactly when the perfect temperature has been achieved to deliver exactly the right combination of juicy wholesomeness and smoky wonderfulness.

If there were a bigfoot within a hundred miles, I would not be surprised to see it rummaging through their dumpster late at night as the coals burn down to dim embers.

I devoured my yummy pile of beef scrapings sitting on a tree stump and setting my cardboard plate on an old wire spool in the muddy gravel parking lot just in front of the shack. I may or may not have gone back and ordered more to take with me on my journey, only to stop an hour down the road at a small creek and eat that as well. I believe I identified a small pile of dung near the creek as belonging to a raccoon or other small creature, though it could have been a dog. It certainly was probably not belonging to a large bipedal animal. Or maybe it was, I don't know, I'm not an expert on shit.

Just an hour later, I checked into my bed and breakfast in Elizabeth City. My host directed me to a delightful local coffee shop where I experienced hugs from Jesus in a cup and a healthy portion of Tiramisu. My kind host humored me as I asked about any sightings in the area. He reported that he has never seen or heard of any sightings in the Elizabeth City area or on the Outer Banks. I inquired about the wild horses of Corolla and he said they do in fact see them, and they are in fact quite large, and they do in fact live with very limited fresh water and eat salty marsh grass and woody scrub brush and they do in fact thrive. It seems that I may need to see for myself and I have resolved that tomorrow I will go to the outer banks and search for the horses. If a horse can survive in such harsh conditions, perhaps a bigfoot may also exist in the unchecked wildernesses.

I feel I may be surrounded by sceptics that think my plans are futile. I'll see for myself. After all, it's only the first day of the search. Surely true research deserves some reprimand from the sceptics. How much sweeter will success seem after enduring what I may only at this point call mild doubt. I have ordered some research material and my Amazon notification has informed me that there are several books waiting outside my door for my return. I can search the literature for sightings, I can hunt both literally and literature-ly.

DECEMBER 2, 2021

Today I explored part of the Outer Banks (OBX) in North Carolina. I went north up the coast towards the small town of Corolla. There's nothing but sand and this thick bushy scrub brush about 8 feet tall. Sand dunes, sand, scrub brush, more sand and some short beach grass. Part of highway 12 literally is not paved, it's a 4x4 road that goes miles and miles up the beach. There are occasional small clusters of beach houses, sandy paths leading from the "highway" to the houses and a few small freshwater ponds hidden in dense scrub brush and beach grass. It is possible for a man, and as we found out, also for a horse, to step 3 feet off the sandy beach into the brush and just disappear completely. I chartered a "horse tour" in Corolla so I didn't have to risk getting the Land Rover stuck on the beach (it's a brand new car and I while it's made for off-roading, I wasn't ready yet for it to see any serious action).

This "charter" consisted of a guy in a pickup with a step into the back, bench seats and a rough and ready roll cage. There were seat belts, but buckling up was like strapping yourself to the back of an enraged rhino and cutting across the savannah. My only saving grace was my company for the day. There were 6 older ladies ranging in age from 55 to 85 and together, we all climbed into the back of this truck and strapped in. Our guide drove slower today than he normally would. It was cold on the coast, my light jacket and hoodie were not enough to provide appropriate protection from the cold and the light rain. The oldest of the old ladies was so slight, I feared she would fly out of the back of the truck when we went over the dunes.

Our driver had been driving this tour for 30 years, and while he claimed there were over a hundred horses in these wild lands of brush and sand, we saw only three. He claims there were two more just out of sight, but out of sight doesn't mean we saw them. Even the three that we saw were motionless and for all I know, could have been cardboard cut outs propped up in the brush. We did see loads of evidence of the horses, however, tracks were everywhere on the sandy roads and smelly piles of dung still steamed in the brisk December wind.

One has to wonder if a population of dozens or even a hundred wild horses can find enough food in this salt and sand encrusted landscape, can find shelter from hurricanes and the strong storms that come ashore on this exposed stretch of land; if these horses can step off the beach, into the brush and completely disappear, perhaps, just maybe, a population of bigfoot can also exist in the wilds of the American landscape.

The tour wrapped up, the old ladies and myself returned to our vehicles after two hours in the elements, having traveled miles and covered acres of exposed land, bumpy, tired, cold and ready for food. The driver assured me that he has never seen or heard of anyone in the OBX who has ever seen a bigfoot. But still, given the trouble we had finding horses, I can easily understand why.

I found myself in a local diner called the Chicken Coop, the special of the day was a chicken pot pie and a drink for less than seven dollars. That pot pie was big enough to easily make three meals. The apple pie that I ordered to go with it was nearly half a pie. Breakfast that morning had been at another local diner, the sausage patties had been the size of hamburgers and I was introduced to something called a "southern fried biscuit." This biscuit is a conduit of pure delight. They take a regular homemade baked biscuit which for any other purposes would suffice as being wonderful. But they take this biscuit, they cut it in half, slather butter on the cut sides and throw it on the griddle until it's crusty and buttery on the outside and light and fluffy on the inside. This is forever forward the way I will prepare biscuits.

I decided I'd keep looking for bigfoot and as I drove back to

Elizabeth City to my bed and breakfast, I found myself watching the sunset and watching for enormous lumbering creatures crossing the road in front of me.

That evening, upon the referral of my host, I went downtown by the harbor and ordered something I had never heard of before. I had Southern Pork Face. I believe it may be the best thing I've ever eaten ever – more like the face of God than the face of a pig. I don't even think it was from the face of the pig. Hell, it could have been raccoon for all I know, but whatever it was, it was amazing.

My waitress that night suggested some hikes I might take at nearby wildlife preserves where I might see some more elusive wildlife. She probably has the right idea. I'm not likely to find bigfoot in a diner or local pub, or a coffee shop, or a sandy beach teaming with wild ponies. As she stated "if you're looking for sheep, you go to the farm, if you're looking for gators, you go to the swamp, unless you're looking for eatin, then you look at the menus." Grand advice and I decide tonight I will rest for a day of hiking tomorrow.

December 3, 2021

This morning I experienced those luscious biscuits again at a different diner across town. They are also called skillet biscuits and their crusty goodness is not lost when covered in gravy. I spent today thinking about biscuits and what flavor jam might be best with them. I also ventured down some dark and dreary roads to some secluded swamp land on a protected wildlife preserve.

Cypress swamps are not something I grew up with. Growing up in northeast Kansas, I thought I knew what a swamp was, but I did not. I went hiking in a true cypress swamp. The great trees grow to massive heights and they great tangle of roots often look like great hands reaching into the ground with many fingers. The roots spread underground, but in the swamp, they get flooded out, so they send roots up above the ground so they can breathe. These knobs sticking up are called cypress knees and if you're not careful, they will reach up and grab you as you walk. That's the story I'm telling anyway, I stubbed my toes many times and face planted in the path more times than I'll admit to, tripping on those blasted roots.

I decided it was certainly possible that a very large bipedal creature could live in these swamps. There are acres and acres of wilderness and while the brush was not thick, the trees are massive and it would be very easy for a large creature to remain invisible in such a place. In fact, today I noted that I did not see any wildlife. I didn't hear a single bird, nor a frog, or see a single insect. I did see some poop on the trail, evidence of a raccoon or possum that probably went through in the dark. One of the signs posted along the trail said to watch for alligators and bears. Perhaps it was void of life because it was December and the area had seen a light frost already. It's also possible that any wildlife within a three mile radius was scared away by my screams of pain and frustration as I continued to clumsily trip over the cypress knees.

I have been fortunate in my many travels to be in the right place at the right time to observe many local festivals. There was once a pet festival that was taking place right outside my hotel in Denver; there were many people with pets of all sizes and shapes and species milling around talking, admiring and visiting. I witnessed a lady lose her pet snake in the crowd and several dogs attacking one another. Leashes would have been helpful perhaps. I also happened to be in Manitou Springs, Colorado once when the annual coffin races were taking place. I witnessed many injuries as people put coffins on wheels and rode down the mountainside inside the coffin, with little chance of steering and a great chance of casualty. There are many wholesome festivals around the world that bring communities together. Elizabeth City, North Carolina has its own delightful Christmas lighting festival. I happened to witness it tonight in the harbor. A dozen or so boats adorned with hundreds of lights paraded around the harbor as city folk stood by, admiring, clapping, waving in the dark and finally breaking into Christmas carols.

Finally, the cold set in and everyone departed the harbor and headed home. The boats returned to their moorings and a discarded napkin fluttered away in a blustering cold ocean breeze, disappearing in the darkness. I curled up in my bed and breakfast room for the night and I light the fireplace in the corner, nearly setting the Christmas garland on fire. Disaster averted, I take some time to ponder the customs and culture of the bigfoot.

There are stories from across the US of people being abducted by bigfoot and taken to a place where a family of the creatures lived. They interacted, ate with and eventually escaped, and I'm stuck with the idea that if they exist, bigfoots must have some sort of communities. To support a population, they must have family units, societal hierarchies, social norms, language, customs, culture. Perhaps there are mating rituals unwitnessed by man, super secret handshakes that different groups have with other groups so they can insure it's another group of bigfoots and not humans in costumes on Halloween. Who knows what's out there and how whatever is out there lives. Maybe "lives" is the wrong word. That implies that they are barely getting by; perhaps… "Resides" might be a better choice. Who knows what's out there and how whatever is out there might reside. Research, and I mean rigorous, methodical published research is lacking on the topic. I'm not a bigfoot researcher; I'm not even a smart man. But I'm curious and I wonder about such things that are beyond my experience.

At any rate, tomorrow I return to Virginia and finish packing. I have to coordinate with movers and get my things routed South. I will leave North Carolina, not having found bigfoot, but rather discovering a rich food culture and a recipe for Skillet Biscuits. That has made this trip worth the while. I've seen the beaches of the OBX and the swamps where the Cypress trees try to kill you. I've witnessed a local festival and I've grown in my wanderings about the existence of things outside of my life's narrative. That all makes this trial research run a success.

As I begin what I believe to be the biggest part of my adventure, I will be asking myself several questions in order to frame my experiences and narrow my perceptions. Does the surrounding wilderness contain the space and resources necessary for a human (and thus a bigfoot) to survive with minimal contact with the human society? Might it be possible for a large bipedal creature to survive in the conditions presented naturally in an area? Would there be shelter, food and water available? Without getting into an argument of whether Maslow's Hierarchy of Needs pertains to a bigfoot, it certainly presents challenges when defining the human condition.

CHAPTER THREE

BLUE RIDGE MOUNTAINS

The Storm Pushes Me South

December 12, 2021

Left the Chesapeake Bay two days ago. Made it into the mountains no problem, was hoping to head to West Virginia and into Ohio to see the Mothman Museum. I hit a nasty winter storm and had to turn south. The mountains are shrouded in such thick freezing fog, the car became encrusted with ice and the roads were perilous. I decided for safety reasons to turn south before crossing the mountains. That storm was nothing to play around with.

After a full day of driving, speed suppressed severely by the weather, I found Fairy Stone State Park near the border of Virginia. There's a dig site where you can dig for fairy stones, a cool crystalline stone that naturally forms in knots and cross shapes. I found a couple in the park gift shop. The muddy red clay at the dig site yielded nothing but crimson stains on my shoes.

There were miles of trails to be walked. I did my best to make it up the muddy slopes and down the slippery leaf covered paths. I found an abandoned mine in the side of the hill, a perfect place for a bigfoot to shelter in – except for the metal gate in front of the entrance. I barely saw a squirrel or bird as I huffed and puffed up and down the mountain sides. There was plenty of brush for cover and an abundance of tree nuts, (walnut, chestnut and hickory). If Bigfoot might be a nut and berry eater, he could possibly survive here. There were nearly-dormant blackberry bushes everywhere along the trails.

The lack of visual contact with any wildlife is probably because I'm old, chubby and having lived at sea level for the past three years, not acclimated to the altitude. That's my excuse anyway. I realize the Blue Ridge Mountains are not very tall and the difference in oxygen levels halfway up the mountains is probably not much different from sea level. But you know what? I struggled. I breathed noisily, I slipped and slid all over those muddy paths and I didn't see a darn thing. Most likely everything alive out there saw me first (or heard me first) and took cover. I did see some beautiful waterfalls, streams and lakes. I ate a ham sandwich next to a bridge over a small stream that emptied into a lake all next to a narrow blacktop road without lines on it. I watched as a fisherman waded out into the stream to fish. Apparently, I ate too noisily too, he didn't catch anything.

Mostly I was happy to be alive and NOT further north where I had planned to be. I could have been snowed or iced in for a few days up there. The reports coming across the radio were not good and while I wanted to go explore there, I realized that heading south was the right choice.

What I did discover could only be described as localized commercial delicacies. One of the best parts about travelling is stopping in small service stations and looking at the snacks and foods available. I found caramel corn flavored potato chips today and Boston Crème Pie Honey Buns. It made me think of when I was growing up in Kansas, we always had Twinkies, but once in a while, someone would come back from Colorado and bring Choco-Diles – which were nothing more than off brand Twinkies dipped in chocolate. We thought they were delightful because they were new and novel. I suppose it's the same here – these strange items are the norm, but they were new and novel to me. I LOVE trying new and wonderful things, even if they seem mundane and pedantic.

Late afternoon I crossed the Blue Ridge Mountains and went by a pass called Lover's Leap. It was so foggy and windy that I could barely see the lines on the road. I had to stop often and manually clear the windshield. The wipers just wouldn't do the job. It's possible that a bigfoot could have been just a couple feet away from me as I stopped on a mountain road to get out and wipe the freezing fog from the windshield. That concealing fog could have hidden a freight train. The wind was so loud and the fog so thick, it's impossible to know what I drove right past on the way.

CHAPTER FOUR

TENNESSEE

THE CAVE AND BBQ AND MUSIC (OF COURSE)

JUST OUTSIDE THE TOWN OF Sweetwater, Tennessee there is a cave adventure and a small pioneer village – tourist attraction. It's a small mountain town on the other side of the Blue Ridge Mountains from whence I had come. The Lost Sea Adventure is a lake at the bottom of a cave system. It's dark and cold and dark and did I mention it's dark down there? It's dark down there. You enter next to the gift shop after walking through an old timey log village full of little shops meant to make money off the tourists that come through. The only thing open was the glass blowing/ jewelry shop. I did make a purchase, it was a fun little shop. But that was before the cave… the cave is entered through a small building, where of course you have buy your ticket. You then go down a very large, very long tunnel where you meet your guide.

This cave served as a meeting place for Native Americans long ago – there is still soot on the ceiling and some drawings and carvings in one of the larger chambers of the cave left from when the various tribes of the area would use the cave for meetings and celebrations and shelter from severe weather. At the bottom of the cave is a lake. Years ago, the park service stocked the lake with rainbow trout thinking the trout would leave the cave through an underground river and they would trace where the trout came out. However, the trout stayed. The water goes somewhere. There's a river that runs into the cave and it's not filling up with waters, so obviously it goes somewhere. At first I thought I had solved the bigfoot mystery with this cave. Surely a cave with a fresh supply of water could support a bigfoot population. The rural hills and low mountains right outside could surely supply enough food for a large population of bigfoots. The cave could be shelter. But as we descended into the darkness of the cave, I quickly realized that bigfoot was gonna need a lamp, a flashlight, or a torch to get very far into the cave. Did I mention it was dark down there?

Once you get to the bottom of the cave where the lake is, the tour guide takes you and your group onto a boat. The lake is lit from beneath with huge flood lights and the trout swim right up to the boat. It's a nice tour but it's one hell of a trek back up and out of the cave. My guide informed me that he had never seen or heard of anyone seeing a bigfoot in or around the cave or anywhere else for that matter. I know more than him on the subject, however. Just two weeks ago, three miles down the road, a drunken motorist hit a large bipedal animal on the very highway the cave adventure was on.

I drove down the road, the forests on either side are thick and I can easily see how something large might be hiding just inside the tree line out of view.

After partaking in some amazing local barbeque at a place call Bradley's Pit Barbecue and Grill, I decided to reroute my trip and head further south to avoid another storm that was already flooding parts of Kentucky, where I was supposed to go next. Alabama, a recent Hogzilla sighting, and a small lake where there have been many bigfoot sightings was next on the agenda. By "next," I mean after a long drive and some human cultural exploration.

As a general rule, I avoid interstate travel. However, sometimes when your plans change and you have to improvise, you find yourself bumper to bumper with enormous trucks in the rain going 80 miles per hour through the mountains. Maybe, just maybe bigfoot has it right. Bigfoot don't mess with traffic. Bigfoot don't get 'n the interstate. Bigfoot doesn't get high blood pressure and white knuckles trying to get to his destination. If I had to make a guess, I'd say bigfoot isn't a destination traveler. I believe he's more interested in the journey, the adventure, the things he might see along the way, rather than being in such a hurry that he can't take in the absolute beauty of his surroundings.

The interstate took me to Nashville. I've never been before, so I figured a quick trip through might be worth it. I can tell you one thing for certain; my guide at the Musician's Hall of Fame was irritated when I asked if he thought bigfoot might have opposable thumbs and thus be able to play guitar. It almost seemed like all he wanted to talk about were musicians, not hypothetical cryptic creatures that may or may not exist. I'm fairly certain that bigfoot would avoid Nashville. I think I will from now on as well. I'm not a musician, I don't care for country music as a preference, and I don't care for the people. Not that I don't like people, I don't, but I don't like crowds most of all. Traffic, crowds, people... so exhausting.

I get it Squatchy, I get it. Avoid the crowds, stay on the back roads. Don't get caught in traffic, don't get tied down by reservations.

Speaking of reservations, I've rented a cabin back in the woods for the night. I'll have to cross into Alabama to get there, though I think the cabin actually sits in Tennessee. The back roads are um… well, they are back there. They don't show up on GPS, the directions to the cabin literally read "if you still see road signs, you're on the wrong road."

CHAPTER FIVE

ALABAMA

CABIN IN THE WOODS AND
SMALL TOWN BARBECUE

DECEMBER 15, 2021

MANY MILES OFF THE HIGHWAY, I found my bed and breakfast that allows you to stay in a rather primitive cabin in the woods. Ok, it wasn't very primitive. It had wifi and hot water. But if you wanted heat, you had to haul your own wood inside and light the fireplace. It was really just a large room with a small laundry and bathroom off the back. It was a log cabin, but I think the logs were newer. This wasn't an ancient log cabin, this was a "Glabin." You've heard of Glamping – glamorous camping – now you're heard of a Glabin. For those who want to post on social media about their little adventure in the woods, but at the same time want to enjoy hot coffee, running water and a hot shower.

A small stream runs about 30 yards from the cabin. There's a small trail to get from the front door to the stream. This bubbling brook doesn't so much babble, but more sings a melancholy song as it falls over small rocks and downed trees. The host, who lives a half mile down the road in what I can only describe as a log palace, says there are trout in the stream and promises that I'll see some wildlife during my brief stay. During my first trek to the stream just before sunset I am treated to a family of three deer, a possum and several squirrels.

This is not a dead wood. These woods are teeming with life. I decided to leave a cut up apple on the back patio over night to see if it's there in the morning. (It was gone, but there were no tracks).

In the morning, the stream had some ice forming around the edge. It was chilly, but I still saw a good number of deer and heard a greater number of birds on my way out of the woods. There were hills, trees, streams, and deer all around the cabin. There's no doubt a bigfoot could survive here. I doubt very much that he lives in a Glabin, but I guess it's possible.

After getting lost a couple times trying to find the main road again, I headed toward a small town nearby in Alabama that celebrates bigfoot as part of its culture. There was even a stop along the highway called "The Bigfoot Adventure." I was excited to pull off the highway and visit with fellow adventurers. However, it turned out it was just a zip line over a valley and there was absolutely no guarantee of seeing or hearing or smelling a bigfoot. In fact the guide looked at me funny when I expressed my disappointment. I've been zip lining before when it wasn't 35 degrees out, so I opted to get back in the car and head into town for a local breakfast.

Breakfast did not disappoint! These southern local diners are the absolute best. Bigfoot has never seen such a feast for only $8.99.

From the small town on the border, I went south to a nearby lake where a bigfoot like creature has been seen many times. It's a small reservoir that clearly used to be a "destination." There are picnic areas all around it with decaying shelter houses, slouching restroom buildings and rotted tables. There were what once must have been very beautiful swimming beaches, but now were covered in sand burrs and trash. Clearly human presence at this small lake has diminished. It seems to be a place where perhaps locals come to drink. Perhaps young people come here to party. Perhaps something dark has happened here. I don't know, it was cold and I suddenly felt like heading further south.

There's a narrow well-kept back road called the Natchez trail. I don't know the story of the road, and I was too lazy to do the research on it. I just saw that it cut clear across Alabama and went all the way to Natchez, Mississippi on the Mississippi river.

This little back road runs through the most beautiful parts of Alabama and just before I got to Mississippi, I ran into a small town where I decided to stop for lunch.

PART TWO

AN AWAKENING

CHAPTER SIX

NEEDS OF THE BODY – LISTEN AND LEARN

A FEW MONTHS PRIOR, I HAD an interesting conversation with a coworker. She was telling me that she had gone to listen to this person of "science" who came to her church to speak. This person had told them that if they listened, and I guess she means REALLY listened to their bodies, their bodies would tell them exactly what it needed for health, balance and well-being. I thought about it and I decided it was probably a bunch of bullshit. However, today I listened to my body when I stopped for gas at this very small town right around lunch time. The smell of an open barbecue pit was abundant. That juicy wood fired smell of dripping meat spoke to me. Today, I thought about what my coworker had said and I listened to my nose. If bigfoot eats barbecue and if there were such a creature within a dozen miles, it must be drawn to this little hole-in-the-wall establishment.

This small restaurant that didn't show up on my GPS and was labeled only with a hand painted sign "BBQ" was run down and dirty. The floors had once been white, but now were the color of the shoelaces in my hiking boots. The tables were covered in dusty old red tablecloths and then with a sheet of plastic that was sticky and looked like someone spilled cigarette smoke on it. My stomach spoke and I listened. The pillar of smoke from the open pit behind the building was the tell-tale sign of a quality piece of pig. I parked in the back and was amazed that such a run-down little place had so many cars in the front. There were people everywhere.

I waited my turn and my stomach decided that I needed the pork rib tips. My coworker would be proud of me I decided as I collected my greasy grocery bag. Looking at the state of the tables, I opted to eat outside by the car. I pulled a folded lawn chair from the back and ate what I can only describe as belly scratches from an angel, in utter silence. This was the south as I imagined it. Small towns, friendly folk, amazing food, eating outside in December, waving to the locals who walked by on their way to get their lunch. Several asked me what was good today, I told them what I was having and they smiled and nodded, knowing they too would soon be in pork laden bliss. Listen to your gut, it knows what you need.

I admire the small towns where you can afford to eat at a local diner without going bankrupt, and where you can ask the gas station attendant about bigfoot without being ridiculed (he hadn't seen any, but his brother's uncle-in-law shot one about six miles outside town by the old quarry).

Life here meanders like the highway that curves through town, forcing you to slow down and take in the local fare. People wander around, slowly, but with direction. They know where they are going, they just aren't in that big of a hurry to get there. Traffic stops when a stray possum or raccoon wanders into the road. The locals speak a little slower, breathe a little deeper and seem to enjoy what their town has to offer, as limited as that may be. There's something to be said about the way of life here.

Perhaps someday I'll become a local somewhere. I'll drift into retirement and mosey down to a local diner for two meals a day. I'll sit on my front porch and watch the fancy cars drive by and know that I used to be in one of those. Perhaps bigfoot will wander into my back yard that will border the woods. After a heavy rain, the small brook in the woods will be heard from my back kitchen window. Wild flowers will bloom and the breeze will mix their fragrance with the sweet perfume of an open pit barbecue place just down the road where they got Hogzilla on a spit.

While this slower pace of life may create a line at the register of the local grocery store, it's ok because it gives you the opportunity to catch up with neighbors. Getting out of the fast lane and into this friendly-driven way of life seems like medicine for the soul. Maybe bigfoot has it right after all. The fewer people the better. One does not need a vast population for survival. I mean, that makes the gene pool a bit shallow, but I am after all in Alabama.

This simpler, slower way of life seems closer to nature, closer to life itself, far removed from the hustle and bustle of huge cities. And while your internet ordered deliveries (if they have that "world-web" here) may take a bit longer to arrive and you probably can't get an Uber or order DoorDash, it may be worth it to force oneself to slow down a bit, live in the moment, get out of the house, and interact with one's community. I'll have to circle back to that. For now, I have to get back on the road, explore the wilds of America, and look for more local fooderies. Oh, and I almost forgot, I'm looking for Bigfoot too.

CHAPTER SEVEN

RURAL AMERICA'S MATING CALL

MISSISSIPPI

I GREW UP IN KANSAS, WENT to college in Nebraska and have lived in many rural areas. I've spent over 3 decades living in rural communities. I have known the peace of leaving my door unlocked when I left for work and not being concerned. I have known smell of a dusty backroad and of brome being cut during hay season. I have known struggles of driving 40 minutes to the nearest store. I have known the difficulty of finding decent coffee.

Not all small towns are desolate, cultureless villages where Wi-Fi is unheard of. Many small towns have developed their own culture, they have thrived and produced young people able to thrive in both small towns and large cities. These young people often move away for opportunities, but some come back home, bringing something of great value with them and resettle, revitalize and re-inhabit the small towns of their upbringings, or they seek out other small towns in which to thrive.

These young people appreciate the quiet quaintness of small

towns, but still recognize the need to have tourists, culture and income from outside the city limits. A "visit-able" small town is a wondrous place. It's a fine line to walk, to make your city, town or village somewhere that people want to visit but still being able to inhibit growth enough to keep the small town feeling.

Nestled on the banks of the Mississippi river is a small city called Natchez, Mississippi. The bulk of the town sits upon a hill or bluff, or just high bank, overlooking the river. From my room in the Natchez Grand Hotel and Suites, I could watch the bald eagles flying over the river. There were quaint little bars, cafes and coffee shops lining the small town streets. There were houses that were two hundred years old next to houses that were modern and sleek. The mix of traditional and contemporary was beautiful. There were pleasant parks, plenty of parking, front porch swings, and outdoor eating at most eateries. Even in December, the weather was gracious enough to allow for alfresco dining. A walk along the river under the magnificent magnolias yielded better views of the wildlife.

There are wild places that come right up to the city. Bigfoot could be a dumpster diving diva in most of these small towns and no one would even know. I spent an extra two nights here, just looking at the town, taking in the mix of architecture, drinking the coffee, strolling the streets, stepping into little shops, sitting down for coffee and a midafternoon croissant. I've made a note to revisit this quaint town during tourist season to see if the streets have become overcrowded, or if it just maintains this quiet slow lifestyle year round.

These small towns have a mating call. It's like elevator music that you hear in waves as you walk down the street. The music slips out of through open doors of ice cream shops, coffee shops, local eateries and antique shops. This call is probably lost on most people. To me, it's like a siren's call. If I'm not careful, I'll end up crashing into a small town during an adventure, unable to leave, helpless and spending the rest of my days in utter bliss sipping coffee on the veranda, strolling under the magnolias and live oaks, watching the eagles and enjoying life.

I wonder if bigfoot has a mating call. I wonder if a bigfoot were to venture into a small town one Tuesday afternoon and sip coffee while nibbling a fresh cranberry – orange muffin, if it would stay. I wonder if it would appreciate the architecture or the music or the hardness of the concrete. Would bigfoot adventure out of his or her wilderness? Would they venture out of their comfort zone? Would they put their suitcase down on a bed and unzip it, wondering if they should unpack it or not? I rarely know when I check into a hotel if I'll be leaving in the morning or seeking to extend my stay. I like that ability to not have to choose all the time. I'm certainly not a destination traveler most of the time, it's all about the journey. It's all about exploring, eating, sitting, watching, observing, noting, writing, reading, listening, walking and living in the moment. I try not to force the experience of a moment. I can only imagine in that way I have common ground with bigfoot. Live in the moment my squatchy brethren, dance in the rain, look at the stars, ponder the big questions, throw stones in the lake, drink the coffee and eat the damn cake!

CHAPTER EIGHT

LOUISIANA

DECADENCE, SWAMPS AND GATOR TAILS

I'D COME TO THE END of my cross country move. House hunting and settling in became the next priority. The adventure and the hunt was far from over. I didn't realize how much of an adventure still awaited in the coming year.

DECEMBER 18

I have reached the city of New Orleans and found a hotel on base in which to reside for the next month while I procure housing. The small base at Belle Chasse sits on a swamp. Drainage canals have been dug and trails paved along side them. Alligators sit along the banks, or in the water, even though it's mid December. Ferns grow everywhere, clinging to bricks, walls, roofs, trees and rocks. Moss thrives in this sub tropical climate. The air is thick and wet. It's like air you can wear. Spanish moss drips from enormous live oak trees. The water is stagnant, thick, dirty, green, and smells of pond mud.

There are armadillos rummaging in the ditches, a huge variety of birds both big and small foraging in open fields. Mostly, what I notice is the trash.

I arrived just a couple months after hurricane Ida. Roofs of buildings are covered in great blue tarps stretched to keep out the winter rains. Trees and fences have been blown over and debris is everywhere. Mostly, however, I notice the trash in canals, in the tree lines, on the fences and in gutters. I realize that it's left over debris from flooding and high winds, but it's dirty and first impressions aren't great.

There are many wildlife preserves around. Barataria, Bayou Savage, Woodland Park, and others. I've hiked them all by now and I am convinced that if a bigfoot could kill and eat an alligator, he could easily raise his family here. The swamps are thick with palmetto palm and all measure and means of other foliage I can't even start to identify. I've noted acres of wild raspberry bushes in Woodland Park. There are many places where the ground is covered in nut shells, I can not identify these trees or the nuts that fall from them, but if they are not poisonous, then surely they represent a feast for a large family of squatches.

DECEMBER 24, 2021

Christmas will be spent doing research. I have no family here and no time to head to Kansas this year to visit. I'm exploring New Orleans proper. I have resigned to find housing on what is known as the West Bank. It's still part of New Orleans for tax purposes, but its really Old Aurora, Algiers, Gretna, Terrytown, Belle Chasse, and other smaller municipalities. Some of them have been annexed by the city of New Orleans, others have not. Since I've decided to live on this side of the river where houses are cheaper and crime is much, much lower, I've also decided to be a tourist in the big city.

This is not my first time visiting New Orleans. But the first time was rushed and somewhat blurry by the time I reached the end of Bourbon Street. There are parks here big enough to hide entire eco systems and about a thousand muggers. If it weren't for the latter, I'd say there could be a family of bigfoot in any of them, living without disruption in deep groves of live oak trees. By now, any bigfoots would have been robbed of their feet.

Moving away from the parks, I honed in on the famous French Quarter. There are numerous back allies and side streets that rival any medieval town of Europe. There are small shops, cafes, creperies, or as I like to call them "crepetoriums," along with small churches, chapels, courtyards and fountains. The quaint spaces invite the foot traveler to all sorts of indulgences. You can buy a beer from one bar, and drink it in another while you listen to music in a third. You can have coffee on a side street bench while listening to a street performer making your ears bleed. You can be both accosted and charmed by a homeless couple while an old man tells you stories and his partner picks your pocket. I suppose that's what New Orleans is really all about; having your king cake and eating it too.

One should experience the Big Easy, Crescent City once or twice. You can take your pick of public transport: the street car, the city bus, the ferries, taxis, or rent-a-bikes. You can pick your pastry as well: beignets, king cake, crepes, donuts, or croissants. Everything is available and if you don't find what you're after, just meander down another street and you're bound to find it. The people are friendly as well; you can show your titties on almost any street in exchange for beads or directions to the nearest deli. My newly tanned nipples did not, however, produce any information about bigfoot.

If bigfoot makes his way into the French Quarter, he may get some delicious treats, but he better wear some shoes; the streets smell of piss and piles of human excrement are present. The cobblestones and bricks are sticky with spilt beer and one can't always tell if he's walking through a puddle of stagnant water, or a pile of vomit. This city has a charm quite literally unlike any other I've ever seen. I believe living on the other side of the river is probably a good thing for my anxiety, my personal property and my sanity in general.

CHAPTER NINE

BATON ROUGE, LOUISIANA

THE SUGAR MILL

JANUARY 11, 2022

I HAVE A HOUSE UNDER CONTRACT, I should close around the end of January of early February. Having hiked many of the parks and preserves local to New Orleans (NOLA), and knowing I won't be taking any extended road trips for a bit, I've decided to take a long weekend in Baton Rouge. I found a bed and breakfast called the Sugar House. It's 200 year old plantation house on the grounds of what used to be an enormous sugar plantation. The entire place has been converted to an organic micro farm. Many acres of the plantation on the banks of the Mississippi River have reverted back to natural woodlands.

I have booked a room for three nights in the servant's quarters of the plantation house. My room backs up to the woods and a pond. There are reports on this plantation of bigfoot (or something like that) encounters going back 150 years. The last one was over 75 years ago before they put the nearby overpass in. I was still excited to visit with the hosts, their family has owned the sugar mill for 5 generations. This is investigative reporting at its best.

I checked in via "contactless" registration. COVID still has it's grip on the country and my hosts don't believe in risking it. The cleaning regimen is pretty strict. I'm to message them and let them know if I need anything. I'm to enjoy the grounds, but not the big house. I'm to put any laundry needs outside my door where they will be picked up while I'm out and new towels and linens will be dropped just inside the door. I'm to message them when I check out. I guess sitting down over coffee for bigfoot stories is probably asking to much.

Regardless of the solitude from my hosts, I've still resigned to take a good walk around the acres of grounds to see if it might be possible for a bigfoot to still exist here.

JANUARY 12, 2022

Trying to walk around the grounds here is completely impossible unless you have a chainsaw and a machete and a gallon of bug repellant, not to mention snake proof boots. I managed to find a field road that went to the back of the property, but two rattlesnakes and a cottonmouth later, I returned to my room ready to explore the city. If bigfoot ever lived in this area, he had his work cut out for him. That brush is thick and everything in there wants to kill you.

After deciding the swamp walk was a wash, I headed to the botanical gardens. In the middle of Baton Rouge, the well-manicured grounds of the botanical gardens are desperately beautiful, even in January. Acres of gardens and woodlands, trails, wildlife and unadulterated beauty. I could only imagine that a bigfoot family living in this place must be the more posh of the squatch species. This place is pristine, easy to get around in and just down right nice. I half expected to see a squatch in a lawn chair hanging out on one of the woodland trails.

Having struck out in the capital city, I returned to my bed and breakfast tired and ready to rest and return home. I took the time to sip some coffee in the gardens of the plantation. I strolled through the courtyard by the fountain. I picked fresh cumquats off the tree by the path and quickly realized they were too sour to go with my coffee. A feeling of reflection hit me and I stopped to examine my journey thus far.

PART THREE

FINDING A PLACE IN THE THICKETS OF IT

CHAPTER TEN

REFLECTIONS AND FORKS

I T'S TIME TO TAKE A minute to look at where I've come from, what I've seen and to think about what I still want to see. In the beginning, I felt like this was just an excuse to visit some new places along my journey from Virginia to Louisiana. I was moving, craving a road trip, an adventure and really, if I'm honest, looking more for a change in my life than for bigfoot. Bigfoot represented the distraction, something to look for while I figured out what was next for me. In the middle of this adventure so far, I had turned 45 years old. If this isn't "middle age," I don't know what is. I'll be lucky if I see 90, so I'm grasping at life choices, evaluating directions and studying what it is that I want to leave behind when I'm gone. At this point in my life, I'm starting to think about where I want to spend the last years of my life. I'm thinking about what I want to be doing and who I want to be doing it with. This journey was set in motion months ago. I decided to make the most of it. I'm chasing a curiosity that I wish I had chased decades ago. I only realize now that even a decade ago, I probably wasn't in a financial position to chase any curiosities. This trip, this adventure, came at the only time in my life that it could. I'm young enough still to do such things, but

I'm also old enough to have some financial freedom so I can afford such frivolities.

I already know the title of this book and it's not what I thought it might be months ago when I started planning. I don't have to be a smart man to realize that I'm not just looking for bigfoot. I'm looking for myself. I'm looking for places that I think I could survive. This truly has become a self study – using bigfoot as a framing device and self-reflection as a lens from which to peer into my writings, my journaling and my life. I'm at a fork in the road. Do I stop with this interest that has at this point already taken a life of it's own. (I have family and friends already sending bigfoot memes constantly) or do I just ride the wave of squatchology and really complete something truly worth the read?

I've completed my move; I've settled into my new house, full of projects and hard DIY lessons, but I'm not ready to end this wandering, this curiosity and the notion that at this point in the journey, I'm just getting good and started. I should be writing the last chapter right now, but I think I'll move forward. I'm going to be in Louisiana for three years at least. I'm damn well going to spend the first year looking for bigfoot everywhere. I'll spend the other two growing in other ways, improving myself and living life to it's fullest! Speaking of living. I feel the need for an international adventure.

CHAPTER ELEVEN

GREECE AND THE MONSTERS WITHIN

I Went to Greece to Wrestle Bigfoot

Late March, Early April

I've taught English for twenty years. Many of those years, I have taught Greek (and other) Mythology. I'm obsessed with the monsters of all mythology stories. The mighty hero slays the monster and gains favor with so and so and marries so and so's daughter who is a princess or some crap like that. Usually, we just make the argument that the monster was a part of himself. He grew, learned a lesson and by doing so, he slew a figurative monster. He leveled up in life. By defeating the darkness within, he becomes worthy and thus is now qualified to marry the princess. Blah blah blah. You know how it goes. You know how it ends before it begins. It's the very fabric of great story telling; growth, education, learning the secrets of life that the mind was not capable of comprehending until a journey had been taken and cultural horizons expanded. Nobody roots for the static characters.

This trip wasn't about growth, it wasn't about leveling up. This trip was all about rest and relaxation on the sandy beaches of the beautiful country of Greece. This journey was all about strolling through vineyards, and exploring ancient ruins. Enjoying the sunset, loving the food and the weather; this trip was about self-care, not self-reflection and growth.

All that said, I cannot just go to a country with such a history of rich cultural mythology and not explore my curiosities. There's no way I'm flying to Greece on a nine day whirl wind tour and not standing in the amphitheaters where ancient tragedies were performed. There's no way I'm not going to stand on the cliffs over-looking the Adriatic and not think about the story of Theseus and the Minotaur. It would take a thousand Minotaurs to keep me from the Acropolis. The ancient temples beckon me and I explored every single one I saw. I climbed mountains with a torn meniscus, I waded into every body of water I could find. I stood on ancient shores, walked through olive groves that were a thousand years old, and I drank soooooo much wine.

I went for the rest and relaxation, I stayed for the food and I soaked in the culture. I jumped over the ropes at the Temple of Poseidon so I could watch the sun setting between the enormous pillars. I marveled at the Oracle of Delphi and I sat and looked across the land to the bays where ancient wars took place. I walked through the Olympic Arch at Olympia. Not any Olympic Arch... THE OLYMPIC ARCH, the first, the original arch.

As I explored and toured and pondered, I found myself not seeking the rest and relaxation I had come to enjoy. I looked at the mountains, and I could almost see the mythical creatures coming to life. I understood how such beauty and rugged terrain could inspire such horrifying monsters. I began to realize that our imaginary mythological monsters really aren't monsters at all. My professors and teachers were correct in saying that the heroes of old killed monsters that were as much a part of themselves as they were a part of their culture. Our monsters are our own. We either live in fear of them or we make friends with them, or we kill them off. We tell the stories of their arrivals, their dark deeds and even cast blame upon them for our own transgressions.

I feel like this is a lesson I could have grasped without going to Greece. I feel like I already knew everything that I've just confirmed about living and breathing and coexisting with our own beasts and our own mythologies.

To this point in my life, I had never considered that I have my own mythology. Mythology is more than a collection of myths. It's a collective of paradigms, views, ideologies and beliefs that come together to form your personal narrative. The monsters in my life are ever present, hidden in shadows but ever tickling my bare feet that hang off the bed in the night. My narrative is my own. No one else can truly write it. Each of us have a narrative that we add to a collective of the community and society that we choose to live in. We identify ourselves, we are identified by others, we add to the societal mythology with our own bits and pieces, cut and hewn by our own experiences, and perceptions. We choose, however, what part of our narrative we openly give out, and by doing so, we control our personal mythologies. Others, however, are free to write their own versions of my narrative as they see fit. I may never know how others perceive me and I do not even care. They are free to create their own mythologies and I may very well be the monster in many narratives.

I know damn well that many people that have crossed the paths of my life are monsters in my narrative.

Let's be realistic. The biggest monster in my story is myself. All my fears and insecurities come together to scare the hell out of me on a regular basis. Am I the hero that kills the monsters? Am I to remain a static character in my own life? Shall I never change? Shall I never grow or learn or express a desire to be more than I am right now?

I think I'm more likely to become one of those people who accepts my monsters as being a part of my psyche and learns to harness them for the strengths they inherently come equipped with. It's not a non-conforming idea to become more than you are struggling to be by learning to live with who you are. By Zeus, that monster under my bed will no longer be tickling my feet in the middle of the night. That bitch will be giving me foot massages.

And that, ladies and gentlemen is a moment of personal growth. That is self-care.

CHAPTER TWELVE

MISSISSIPPI AND THE GULF COAST

THE SAND SQUATCH

MAY, 2022

WITH A TRIP TO GREECE behind me, I'm back to exploring with renewed vigor. I planned a trip to Gulfport, Mississippi, knowing I would take highway 90 which will take me right out on the beach at Waveland and will take me along miles of sandy paradise through Bay St. Luis, Pass Christian, Long Beach and into Gulfport. A couple weeks in the sand can never hurt. I planned some hiking a bit inland for research purposes, but mostly, I'm exploring the idea of food. Can Bigfoot live on seafood? Would a bigfoot be able to procure mass amounts of gulf shrimp, crayfish, and other sea creatures? There are also wild boar inland a bit, perhaps if he enjoys some pork butt as much as I do, he might be hunting there.

There's a small local chain of seafood places called "Shaggy's." There is one in Pass Christian that I always find myself driving by at meal times. The place overlooks a small harbor where fishermen moor their boats. The food is amazing, the atmosphere terrific, the outdoor seating with pelicans trying to steal your food right off the table is adventurous. I could sit there all day, watching the birds, the fishing boats and the waves. But there's sand to sit on, a tan to acquire and serious questions to ponder.

I'm staying in Gulfport, exploring the small town feel of this city. Gulfport is like the little brother of Biloxi. The spoiled younger brother that got everything he wanted his whole life. It's a quaint little city with a beautiful downtown. There are shops and café's, bars and coffee shops, pizza places, steak places, seafood places and outdoor seating almost everywhere. I'm content to grab a coffee and write until it's time to walk next door to the deli where I can eat a sandwich and write until it's time to go next door for ice cream and then back to the first place for coffee and more writing.'

I went inland to a hiking trail through a sort of park that led to a river. The mosquitoes were crossed with Californian Condors and after just half an hour, I swear I needed a blood transfusion. I made it to the river where there were three young men sitting on a log. They were possibly out of high school, but possibly barely able to drive. I startled them as much as they startled me. The trail did not seem as though it had been walked today. I did not expect to see anyone. They seemed to be expecting someone, but it was very clear from their expressions when I stepped into the clearing that I was not what they were expecting. To avoid a complete awkward moment, I made a pleasant salutation and a comment about the mosquitoes and I hurried back the way I came from.

On my way to the car, I met the second surprise of this hike. A lady, of undetermined age, wearing clothing better suited to a dark street corner behind the waffle house than hiking through the brush. Her make-up was rushed and her bare fish net stockings were snagging on every loose bramble along the trail. She was clearly looking for someone, but it wasn't me. She kindly asked if I knew which trail led to the river and I pointed in the direction I had just come from.

I ran the rest of the way to the car. I didn't need to be implicated in the finding of a dead hooker back in the trails by the river. It was as I was driving back to the city of Gulfport that I thought about a new business model. What if someone developed an App for your phone where you ordered a hooker delivery? I even reached out to a couple friends on the way back to the hotel about what the name of that app might be? Hookerhub? Whoredash? It was a funny scenario to play out in my head, but also human trafficking is no laughing matter.

I left Gulfport today to explore some botanical gardens further east and north. Walking around the gardens is always a delight. The Bellingrath Gardens and Home in Alabama backs up to the Fowl River. The buildings and trails guide the visitor through a maze of greenhouses, grand plazas, beautiful vistas and wooded paths. There was an alligator in the big pond at the gardens today and there were signs posted to stay clear. The home on the estate overlooked the river from atop a small hill, waterfalls, and lush bedding plants created a heavenly place to spend an afternoon. Even in the afternoon, May humidity and sweltering heat, everything was enjoyable.

From Bellingrath Gardens, I made my way to Dauphin Island, Alabama. It's not a large island, but it has some amazing beaches. There was a storm rolling in off the gulf, so I didn't stay for the sand. I found myself holed up in a bakery next to a coffee shop as the dark clouds passed over dumping buckets of hot rain on a mass of tourists. I did make some conversation with some locals, none of which believed that anything even resembling a bigfoot has ever been seen on or near the island. I picked up some drift wood from the causeway leading out to the island, and I met one of the island's most terrifying wild creatures. By that I mean I stumbled into a nest of fire ants. When I tell you that fire ants will go straight for the nuts in a down and dirty bar fight, I mean, they immediately swarm your legs and don't stop until they reach your waistband of your undies.

Nursing a hundred or more fire ant bites, I headed back to Gulfport to spend a couple days resting and recuperating. I took the back roads back and even though I was in some serious pain from my battle with the red demons of Dauphin Island, I still stopped at a couple roadside stops beside some cypress swamps to get out, stretch, (and mostly to scratch) and search from the picnic tables for a large hairy bipedal creature that might be enticed to come close by the smell of fresh baked goods from the bakery. I finished my coffee and my snacks and headed back to the safety of a hot soak in the bath with what the pharmacist insisted would be the most luxurious anti-itch bath I would ever have. It was decent. The pool seemed to be more relief and by night, I was able to write and then sleep in relative peace. I could only imagine what would happen if Bigfoot got into a nest of fire ants. Would they burrow into his hair and sting or bite and cause as much discomfort? Or would his hair or fur be thick enough to repel the small warriors?

I spent the next couple days lounging on the beach, exploring downtown, sitting by the pool and generally just being lazy. Still reeling from my defeat by the fire nation, I mean the fire ants, and the mosquito condors the day before, I basked in the sun and added a sunburn to my list of injuries.

Feeling utterly defeated by nature, I set out for home. It's just an hour's drive on the interstate, but we established months ago that it seems unlikely to see a bigfoot on the interstate. I'll spend an extra 45 minutes on the road to avoid the traffic on the interstate. I'll spend my $2 to take the Lower Algiers Ferry too, instead of driving through New Orleans proper and taking that silly bridge across the Mississippi.

CHAPTER THIRTEEN

THE FAMILY THAT HUNTS TOGETHER STILL DOESN'T FIND A SQUATCH

LATE MAY

I HAD NOT BEEN TO KANSAS to see my immediate family since my mother passed away in March of 2021. COVID and a busy work and travel schedule had hampered any plans I had tried to make to go back. When one of my brothers decided to come down for a visit, I found myself overly excited. He, his wife and their daughter made the trip down and we did everything. We went on a swamp tour. Deep in the bayou, we still didn't see any traces of bigfoot. We saw some gators though!

We took the two hour drive down to Venice, LA, where the road basically runs into the water and doesn't come back out. We spend half an hour at a small pull over in a cypress swamp. As soon as we stepped out of the car, the gators came swimming towards us. It's clear that these gators were used to being fed here, perhaps by bigfoot, more likely by locals.

We ate barbecue and seafood and we even went downtown New

Orleans. There was no expectation of finding bigfoot in a gutter just off bourbon street, and it seemed unlikely to find him sleeping on a park bench at the park. If you're never been to New Orleans and you leave, having not been to the French Quarter and seeing some of the more famous tourist traps, well, you're not really living are you? But seeing how those tourist traps are not our cup of tea, we did our due diligence and stopped but quickly found ourselves exploring local nature preserves and parks.

I'm sure my family thinks my bigfoot obsession is a bit off, but they don't really say anything about it. They play along, they point at things in the trees that aren't there, they look at the landscape and ask questions about whether a bigfoot could eat that enormous snake crawling across our path or whether he would leave it alone. They joke about my coffee being strong enough make bigfoot walk a tight rope and they goad me a bit when we see places in the brush where something large recently went through. I don't mind. It's become a pretty good inside joke with several friends and family.

Most everyone has the same reaction when I tell them I'm searching for Bigfoot. Eyebrows raise, voices quiver a bit and they ask a few obvious questions, but those closest to me just shrug and nod and move closer to the diagnosis of bat-shit crazy. But then we see some cows along the highway and someone says "My Cows" and I silently think, I bet bigfoot probably has a heard of cows too. And we all smile and pull into the parking lot of the barbecue place. We eat until we got the meat sweats and then we pack up the leftovers and head back to the house for naps.

I can't think of a better way to spend time with family than trudging through the woods, working on the house a bit while I have the help, and hanging out under the carport, eating, drinking and just being together.

It occurs to me that I almost always think of bigfoot as a solitary creature, meeting up with other bigfoots for conjugal visits in a sexy, romantic moon-lit clearing. But maybe bigfoot likes hanging out with his family. Maybe he has close bonds and calls them or at least texts them every week or so. Maybe bigfoot has a carport with a crystal chandelier like I do and he and his family sit there talking about the old days, drinking a beer, and gnawing on leftover brisket.

Maybe that's what my story has been missing, an element of family. A deepness of close friendship with a blood relative. Maybe I need to go back to see the fam more. Nothing says I can't and won't look for bigfoot on the way! After all, I have to cross the Ozark Mountains to get back home from here, there's the Ozark Howler I can look for. Bigfoot has a long history of sightings in the Ozarks anyway, so maybe since my brother and his fam did a poor job searching on the way down here, I'll have to plan my own trip. Bigfoot must surely get a little lonely sometimes and miss his family?

CHAPTER FOURTEEN

A LONG REFLECTION – LOOKING INTO LIFE'S POOL (AND REALIZING IT'S A BIT OF A CESSPOOL)

SUMMER IN NEW ORLEANS IS a time and place I don't want to be anymore. I always thought I knew what humidity was. I could never have been more wrong. I grew up in a four season part of the country. New Orleans has "Summer" and then it has the rest of the year where the temperature sways between cool and hot with a day of cold here and there followed by a day of hot. I've done my best to use the humid summer to explore more, but mostly I spent it sitting around with a sweaty swampy ass crack.

All of this travel, all of this eating and driving and riding and looking and exploring has reaffirmed some beliefs that I already had and brought upon a few realizations that I should have already known. Few things should surprise me at this point, but reading over my journal and even this book so far and reflecting on my writings and my thoughts, have yielded a few surprises. I've learned more who I am, who I want to be and mostly, probably more importantly, I've learned who I am not. I think that, as much as anything, is just as important a realization as who I am.

While I don't spend much time outside in the summer because I don't enjoy wearing the air, I do spend a goodly amount of time sitting by the window, sitting in a car, enjoying the green, watching the ever present clouds, and counting the different species of wildlife that comes into view. I don't know that I needed months of reflection, I don't even think I needed months of journaling to know how this story ends.

I didn't find bigfoot. Not a trace, not a hair, not a footprint, not a good story, not anything. What I did find was a bit of myself. I made some realizations about myself. This truly was a study on self and self identity. More than anything, all this writing, rewriting, travelling and editing was an important part of the journey just for the fact that I am now a bit closer to understanding what makes me tick. I now see where I do and do not want to live as I get older. I understand better how I want to live my life, things I still want to do, things I don't want to do. I understand what it is to be me.

I'm not a big city person. I've lived in and around some areas of enormous population density. I've driven on those interstates where you stare at license plates in front of you. I've eaten at those fancy places that require a suit jacket for entry and charge you a fortune for the smallest portions I've ever seen. Those places don't make you cultured, they make you poor and hungry. I've been around the world, I've experienced and explored far off places, but I've never felt at home in any of them. I've always been the wandering soul, and never felt a sense of home. Even going "home" to where I grew up didn't lead to a sense of nostalgia like I expected. It cemented ever more the search for someplace unknown as of yet. I may never find home. I may be nomadic for the rest of my life. But if and when I do set down roots, it won't be in one of those big cities. It won't be where the traffic is stifling. It will be somewhere where the food is good, the portions are big and the views are unobstructed. It will be closer to nature, where green space and blue space dominate over the brown space and the grey space.

CHAPTER FIFTEEN

HUNTING FOR BIGFOOT; FINDING ONLY MYSELF

Q UITE LITERALLY, I'VE TRAVELLED A good part of the world in my lifetime. I've lived in some pretty spectacular places. I've experienced some wonderful things, tasted some wonderful food and I've met some truly amazing people. I've had some incredible experiences, taken advantage of some brilliant opportunities. I've succeeded and I've failed. But always; always I felt like I might be missing something. Not to say I didn't have everything I could possibly want, need and more, but I always felt like there might be something I was missing.

Perhaps the reader picked up early on in this adventure the metaphor that this hunt was to be. I literally hoped to find bigfoot. I actually thought that I might find a trace, a hair, a sign, a track. I believed that this was a hunt for a mystical creature as much as anything.

I've been through my journal a hundred times. I've read and re-read these chapters, I realize now this wasn't so much a journey into the realm of Bigfoot. I am bigfoot, or at least bigfoot is a part of me. This has always been a search into my being, my soul, my very existence. This has been a growth. This has been self-reflection at its best.

I would encourage everyone to take a "walk about" (as my old friend Jen would call it). Call it a gap year, call it a mid-life crisis, call it a wandering, get lost in the woods, get lost in good food, cultural experiences and new places. Most importantly, get lost in yourself. Look past the mirror, look past your upbringing, your beliefs, your shortcomings and your passions. See who you really are, see who you really can be and see who you really are not. How can we possibly expect to find something mystical and mythical if we cannot find ourselves? I may never find an actual bigfoot. I may never find a sign of his existence. It won't stop me from believing. We call it faith. Extend that metaphor as much as you want, turn this into a sermon, turn it into nonsense, but please; please turn it into self-reflection. Find yourself. It doesn't take a journey, a search, a quandary or a hunt. It just takes self-awareness and the ability to believe in who you are, what you are and why you are those things. Its not an easy concept to grasp, but it's the closest any of us will probably come to finding bigfoot. (Unless I hit him with my car someday, then I'll be pretty damn close).

REFERENCES

Alan, Bülent. "Self-Study as a Qualitative Research Methodology in Teacher Education." *Journal of Qualitative Research in Edcuation* (2016).

Coffey, Ron. *Kentucky Cryptids.* Fairy Ring Press, 2018.

Coleman, Loren and Jerome Clark. *Cryptozoology A to Z.* New York: Fireside, 1999.

Hamilton, Mary Lynn, Laura Smith and Kristen Worthington. "Fitting the Methodology with the Research: An exploration of narrative, self-study and auto-ethnography." *Studying Teacher Education* (2009): 17-28.

Lunenberg, Mieke, Fred Korthagen and Rosanne Zwart. "Self-Study Research and the Development of Teacher Educators' Professional Identities." *European Educational Research Journal* (2011): 407-420.

Milner Halls, Kelly. *Cryptid Creatures: A Field Guide to 50 Fascinating Beasts.* Little Bigfoot, 2019.

Redfern, Nick. *The Bigfoot Book.* Canton, MI: Visible Ink Press, 2016.

Printed in the United States
by Baker & Taylor Publisher Services